Minimalist

Easy, practical tips for a healthier, happier life!

J.N. LEE

What Can You Get From This Book?

- Find out how Minimalist Living can give you a healthier, happier life

- Discover practical tips for de-cluttering your home or office

- How saying 'no' can make a big difference

- Why owning less can give you more

- How to quickly and easily adopt a minimalist life (without throwing everything out!)

- The most common mistakes people make (and how to avoid them)

- Practical tips for saving time, money and the planet!

- How redefining 'happiness' can revolutionize your day

- And much more!

The simple aim of this book is to help you unlock the power of minimalist living with simple, practical tips that anyone can use.

Compiled with the input of expert designers, psychologists and top lifestyle coaches this guide is your ticket to easy living through cutting back on the things you don't need.

Whether you are a busy office worker, hoping to change your home or just curious at what can be achieved, you will find powerful tips and techniques to help you boost motivation, increase relaxation and most of all make you happy!

Unlock the power of minimalist living now...

Contents

Minimalist Living Made Simple: An Introduction

We live in an age of consumerism. There is no doubting it.

As we go through life we are bombarded by messages prompting us to buy more in an effort to *be* more. We are told time and time again that the things we own are a sign of who we are and success in life can be measured by the stuff we have.

A big house, several cars and the latest gadgets. All the time we are faced with messages promoting the idea that owning these things leads to happiness and fulfilment.

There is just one problem. None of that is true.

Are you happy and fulfilled right now? If so then I commend you for being in the minority. The majority of us however, find that wanting to own new phones, fancy cars and all the trappings of a luxury lifestyle just leave us feeling hollow and frustrated. Indeed even if, after years of saving, you get your hands on one of these luxuries you quickly find that the excitement and joy wears off.

In fact scientific studies have now shown that we are becoming increasingly resistant to happiness through material possessions and it is taking more and more to sate our mind's desire. A shiny new computer may have made you content for a long time years ago but these days the joy fades as soon as we see a commercial for the newer version. An investigation from Cornell University showed that we adapt quickly to new physical objects and they soon lose their attraction.

So what is the answer?

Minimalism.

Minimalism isn't an esoteric concept and it doesn't involve meditating halfway up a mountain. It has no ties to religion (if you don't want it to) and can be practiced by anyone. Minimalism is simply the act of trimming away the unnecessary in your life and re-programming our brains to take simple pleasure and joy from what we already have. (Instead of constantly seeking the next thing).

Minimalist living, in particular, is a powerful concept that can revolutionize the way you go about your daily life, and give you a happier more relaxed existence. Best of all it requires no expenditure, no complicated training and no hard, physical work. Minimalist living is all about gently adjusting the way you look at your life and the things you own, and tweaking these to bring about a more positive environment.

By de-cluttering, better organization and a few lifestyle changes you can lower stress levels, improve motivation and lead a happier, more positive existence.

It's not just some fairy tale either; the same study from Cornell University also showed that our daily experience and outlook on life is more important to happiness than the stuff we own.

So sit back, relax and discover how, with a few small changes, Minimalist Living can work for you...

What is Minimalist Living?

The choice to assume a simple, minimalist lifestyle is often made in response to problems caused by overconsumption. Materialism may be mainstream, but so are stress, depression, and debt. Minimalists rebel against the norm in the name of diversity, sustainability, economic progress, and social justice.

Despite its simple nature, minimalist living is not easily maintained. Indeed, consumerism is now harder to escape than ever before. Thanks to increasingly effective marketing techniques, the standard of living has risen far above what anyone needs to survive. In this materialistic era, boundaries which might have previously slowed excessive consumerist tendencies are routinely cast aside. Credit allows you to live and spend beyond your means. The focus has shifted from what you need to what you want; and what advertising tells you to want. Lines have been blurred, morphing excessive consumption from a luxury reserved for the rich into the accepted norm for everyone.

You might not be aware of how rapidly expectations have risen over the last few generations. It has happened gradually but steadily. People now expect larger homes, nicer vehicles, more fashionable clothing, pricier technology, and greater levels of comfort. You have been conditioned to believe that these things will bring you joy and happiness. However, the requirements for maintaining such a lifestyle are often too demanding to allow you to enjoy life. In fact, you might be so focused on acquiring the next bigger and better thing that you fail to appreciate any of the wonderful things that you already possess.

Some level of consumption is necessary to sustain life; however it does need not be in excess. Excessive consumption steals the moments of joy that make life worth living. It also robs our planet of vital resources, exploits workers, destroys our environment, creates debt, damages families, encourages addiction, propels obesity, and threatens your health. Minimalists yearn to break free from this ugly cycle.

Minimalist living will help you reclaim a healthy, happy, and independent life through the rejection of consumerism and overconsumption. Minimalists pause before making any purchase or commitment. First, they consider whether it is truly necessary. Then, they determine whether the benefits outweigh the cost in terms of both time and money.

Who is a Minimalist?

There are many ways to gauge your level of commitment to a minimalist lifestyle. You could count the number of objects you own, examine their usefulness, evaluate your home's décor, or compare your level of consumption to your neighbors. You could do all that but it would be a waste of time.

In fact, spending time counting the books on your shelf is the exact opposite of minimalism. Why should you waste time counting books when you could enjoy reading one instead? Minimalism is not really about owning less than you could, but about enjoying everything you have. Instead of asking yourself how many objects you possess, ask yourself whether those things serve a purpose or bring happiness to your life.

Being a minimalist is not about creating clean lines. It is about eliminating anything that distracts you from your purpose whether it is clutter, work, obligations, dependency, or stress. In order to remove obstacles, minimalism asks you to reconsider what you really need to survive and feel fulfilled. It is an awareness that you are not the sum of your possessions and happiness does not come from material things.

Minimalist living advocates owning less not because it is cool or makes you somehow holier than your cohorts, but because buying fewer things frees up space and money. This in turn reduces the number of hours you must toil to support your lifestyle, which frees you to invest your time in personally fulfilling activities.

Practical minimalism is a philosophy that can be applied to your life to reduce stress and make things better. Simple, minimalist living avoids luxury, but that does not necessarily mean cutting out comfort. Instead, it redefines your true needs and provides the means to obtain happiness.

Where Does Minimalist Living Come From?

The minimalist philosophy is not a new one. People who exemplify the minimalist lifestyle have appeared throughout history. Their beliefs have persevered across thousands of years, fluctuating in popularity but never disappearing entirely. Each period is marked by a different brand of minimalism, though the underlying message has remained. At the heart of minimalism is a tradition of simplicity in all aspects of life. Its simple, immaterial virtues have struck a chord with religious and spiritual leaders as well as artists, musicians, philosophers, environmentalists, and writers.

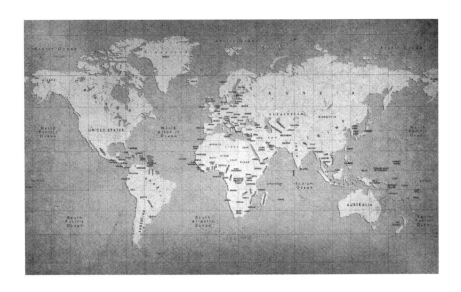

While minimalism has spanned countless cultural and geographic borders, its origins have been traced to the most ancient societies of the orient. The earliest minimalists were the Shramana during the Iron Age in India, Buddha during the 6th century BC, and the Nazirites including John the Baptist of 36 CE. Their most notable leaders include Confucius, Buddha, Zarathustra, and Laozi. These and later minimalists like Ghandi, St. Francis of Assisi, Epicurus, Albert Schweitzer, Leo Tolstoy, Ammon Hennacy and Mother Teresa are still revered today. Their minimalist messages have lingered long after deaths.

The Greek philosopher, Epicurus, identified the route to a happier, more trouble-free life through the maintenance of a simple lifestyle. He observed that those who lived in the lap of wealth and luxury were often plagued by problems that far diminished any benefit of their positions. Many people of the era connected with his message. As a result, Epicureanism saw profound popularity between the 4th century BC and the 3rd century AD. Followers were encouraged to acquire only the basics necessary to maintain life, avoid excess, and practice moderation of all things.

While minimalism is often practiced as a secular philosophy, it has continued to be borrowed by religious organizations for centuries. Many of these religions also shun all money and technology, creating a clear separation between themselves and outsiders. Examples include the Mennonites, Amish, Shakers, Quakers, and Hutterites. In particular, the Quaker society dates back to the 17th century. Their practice of minimalism is rooted in the Testimony of Simplicity, which solidifies their commitment to a simple lifestyle. A similar devotion is demanded by Islamic followers of the prophet Mohammed.

Well-known writer and philosopher Jean Jaques Rousseau encouraged the minimalist movement during the 18th century. Evidence of his strong belief in the value of a simpler lifestyle can be found in many of his works, including his *Discourse on Inequality* and the *Discourse on the Arts and Science*. A similar message was not only written about, but devoutly practiced by well-known naturalist Henry David Thoreau, who spent years living a strictly minimalist and often solitary life in the mid-1800s.

During the Victorian era, Britain saw a surge in the movement bolstered by folks such as Henry Stephens Salt, who preferred the term "Simplification." He was followed by a long line of philosophers, writers, and poets who would romanticize the notion of a more basic lifestyle during the early 1900s. Not the least of these were William Morris, John Cowper Powys, and Patrick Kavanagh.

As industrialization and urbanization began to take hold of Western Society, one group in particular, known as the Vanderbilt Agrarians, fought for minimalism to remain. Though the campaign failed for the most part, their support for a simple, sustainable community was heard loud and clear throughout the southern portion of the United States. Similar warnings against consumerism and materialism were also published by Thorstein Veblen and Richard Gregg. Gregg labelled his version of minimalism as "voluntary simplicity".

While industrialization forged ahead undeterred, a wealth of literary, artistic, and musical works continued in opposition to what they saw as progress in the wrong direction. Urbanization promised easier living but was wrought with kinks, placing more strain on the working class than ever before. The likes of Richard Gregg, E.F. Schumacher, and Ernest Callenbach continued writing to no avail. Sure, they maintained a few followers, many whom preferred to enjoy life on the fringe of society, but on the whole their resistance failed to slow the forward march into the 21st century.

The most noteworthy and recognizable champion of the minimalist cause was born in October of 1869 and lived to spread the values of simple living until January 30, 1948. Gandhi was not a minimalist by necessity or station. He was born into a significantly wealthy family. Gandhi was given the best the world had to offer, including a world-class education. Still, he found that happiness did not lie in excess. He practiced his preaching's in the most literal sense, giving away all of his material possessions in favor of a minimalist lifestyle. At the time of his death, Gandhi is reported to have left behind only a handful of belongings including a watch, glasses, footwear, and a bowl. Gandhi turned simple living into an art form, leaving behind a vast expanse of knowledge and wisdom that continues to inspire many.

Today traditional Buddhist monks continue to practice minimalism. Their impermeable faith in this philosophy touches every aspect of their lives. At the core of their existence is the belief that nothing is permanent, all things change and, therefore, accumulating wealth or holding on to objects is a waste of life energy.

Not all minimalists give away all of their possessions, avoid home ownership, or deny the benefits of financial success. Many enjoy a more practical brand of minimalism that can be applied in moderation. Today's minimalist remains present in modern society while reducing wastefulness, re-evaluating their definitions of happiness, putting emphasis on their priorities, and eliminating unnecessary stress.

The most important aspect of minimalism, supported by all of its heroes from Buddha to Mother Teresa, is the elimination of anything that prevents you from enjoying a fulfilled life.

How Can Minimalism Help Me?

You might be drawn to minimalist living for a wide range of reasons. Perhaps you hope to improve your health, your finances, or your relationships. Maybe are excited to try a new lifestyle. You will be in good company if you are seeking to reduce your impact on the environment, work less, or become more self-sufficient. And you certainly would not be the first to choose minimalism in your quest to gain enlightenment or achieve a greater spiritual connection. The simple philosophy of minimalist living can assist all of these goals and more.

In the barest sense, being a minimalist is to have and use less. Your initial reaction to this sentence might be one of discomfort. Having to give up something doesn't sound especially pleasant. This is because modern life has conditioned you to think in terms of material things. Not everything a minimalist lets go of is a physical object. Minimalist living removes all of the items that are blocking your path to a better life. This means eliminating stress, negative habits, debts, addictions, and clutter. Minimalists give up these chains to gain freedom, peace of mind, security, time, enlightenment, confidence, and love.

For some reason, discussions of minimalist living tend to stall on the rules and expectations. Not enough time is focused on the enjoyment that can be found. While the reasons for adopting a minimalist lifestyle are many, most people continue because it brings a deep sense of fulfilment.

The age old test for separating the optimist from the pessimist is to inquire whether the glass is half full or half empty. Such oversimplification cannot be applied to minimalism. A minimalist might possess half the stuff of a materialist, but they might also experience half the stress and twice the joy. The more things you own, the more time you must devote to cleaning, maintaining, fixing and securing. You will also spend more time working to pay for the initial purchase, taxes, continued maintenance, and required insurance.

Who doesn't want to spend less time cleaning? When you have fewer dishes, there are less to wash. When you have fewer clothes, there is less laundry to fold and put away. When you have fewer Knick knacks and furnishings, there is less to dust to clean and fewer things to organize. When you finish a day of work, your home will be cleaner, more organized, and more inviting. You will feel more relaxed, more comfortable, and more proud.

When you have fewer belongings, there are fewer commitments crowding your time and space. In essence, you become free. Having fewer things not only means you can pay fewer bills and work less often, but you gain the freedom of mobility. You are no longer bound to one place by the bulk of your possessions. Your future becomes a blank slate full of potential opportunities that you are ready and able to accept.

In addition to freedom, you will gain time. Instead of cleaning, maintaining, working, and planning purchases, you can spend your time doing the things that make you happy. You will also notice that you have more money. It is simple math. When you buy less, you have more. This means you can pay off debts faster and eventually maintain a debt-free lifestyle. When it is time to make a big purchase, you will have less stress and greater enjoyment. You will be more confident in your choice. You will know what you need and what you can afford.

Amazing things happen when you free yourself from the urge to 'keep up with the Joneses.' When you adopt a minimalist mind-set, you will no longer feel the pressure to have the newest tech gadgets or wear the most current trends. Instead, you will think in terms of your own personal aspirations. Once your friends and family members recognize your commitments, life will become less competitive. You and your loved ones will be able to separate your self-worth from the things you have. This leads to more authentic and rewarding relationships.

When you approach life with a minimalist mind-set, you become more conscious of your consumption. Consuming fewer resources is better for your health and your environment. Consuming fewer calories can lead to weight loss. Eating nutrition- packed fuel and cutting out unnecessary junk can improve your health and prevent disease. Using less water, gas, or electricity saves you money and decreases the strain placed on natural resources. Buying fewer factory-made items reduces pollution.

Minimalists are good neighbors not only because they protect the environment, but because they leave more for others. There is a limit to the earth's resources. Being painfully aware of this fact, minimalists are happy to use only what they need. This means there will be more available for future generations. Free yourself from the greed that destroys our world and distracts you from everything that is real.

Addiction comes in many forms. Adopting a minimalist perspective will allow you stop and think before giving in to unhealthy impulses. While you may still choose to drink, smoke, gamble, or engage in other bad habits, you will be forced to re-evaluate the role those habits play in your life. Most addictions can be attributed to stress. When you live more simply, you will remove those triggers from your life. At the end of the day, minimalist living means being honest with yourself about your true needs. You might enjoy a cold beer, but do you really need a dozen?

When you escape consumerism, you begin to find renewed joy in the simpler things. Watching a single sunset with someone you love can bring a deeper level of joy than shopping for the latest and greatest. You will find more time for camping, traveling, reading, creating, music, adventure, and sport. You will finally have the opportunity to play pass with your kids or go for a jog. You may question why you wasted so much time working when you could have been laughing with friends and literally stopping to smell the roses. Life is full of natural beauty that doesn't bear a price tag.

Minimalists breathe deeper and sleep better because they are truly living and enjoying life every day. The challenges they take on create eustress, not distress because they have been purposely and wisely chosen. By getting down to the basics, minimalists purge clutter and welcome a more fulfilling life.

You do not have to take on every aspect of your life all at once. Start small; choose one area in your life where you would like to apply minimalist virtues. Start there. In no time it will spread, eliminating stress and improving your outlook at every turn.

"One of the advantages of being born in an affluent society is that if one has any intelligence at all, one will realize that having more and more won't solve the problem, and happiness does not lie in possessions, or even relationships: The answer lies within ourselves. If we can't find peace and happiness there, it's not going to come from the outside."

–Tenzin Palmo, 1943

Creating Your Minimalist Statement

Your minimalist statement is the mission statement for your life. You might think of business when you hear the term "mission statement". Mission statements have long been established as invaluable business tools. Recent research conducted by Gallup, the leading global performance consulting company, confirms that companies with clear mission statements have more productive workers and lower turnover rates.

That said, mission statements are not just for corporations. Creating your own minimalist statement is a great way to identify your goals, create clarity, maintain focus, make better decisions, and stay true to your minimalist lifestyle. In short, your minimalist statement will keep order in a chaotic, materialist world.

While similar in style and function, minimalist statements are not exactly the same as your typical mission statement. In a minimalist statement you will identify your most important goals and paint a picture of success. In essence, you will explain your reason for incorporating minimalism into your life.

Your minimalist statement will establish your direction forward and establish your purpose in life. It will quietly guide you toward your destination. A minimalist statement is also quite different from a new year's resolution. For one, you should write your minimalist statement down. You do not have to share it with others, but you should revisit it often throughout the year.

The other big difference is that your minimalist statement is not a wish or something you hope to do. It is what you are working towards and will accomplish. Minimalist statements are larger and more positive. Your new year's resolution might be to eat more vegetables or lose 10 pounds. These are good goals, but they are not your reason for living.

Minimalist Statement Examples:

- I will work less and have more quality time with my family and friends. I will also be able to devout more time to reading and crafting.

- I will develop more meaningful relationships that will foster personal growth.

- I will be healthier and more confident.

- I will be able to travel anywhere in the world whenever I choose.

- I will live simply. I will enjoy a home that is filled with more natural light and less stuff.

- I will leave cleaner air and more resources for my grandchildren.

- I will have more downtime to sit with nature, relax, and follow my passions.

This book can help you determine what you need to do, but it is up to you to determine why you are doing it. You already have the answer inside you. Stephen Cove, author of First Things First, describes the immense benefits obtained by "connecting with your own unique purpose". In particular, he highlights "the profound satisfaction that comes from fulfilling it."

Write an effective minimalist statement that captures your vision of the future and reflects your personal mission. Anytime you find yourself struggling to determine the best route forward or questioning the point of the journey, return to your statement. Measure your actions against your minimalist statement to determine the right direction to travel next. By creating your statement today, you will draft the compass that will lead you towards a minimalist lifestyle and personal fulfilment.

Getting Started

- Take a moment to ruminate over past successes. Write these down. Is there a common thread?

- In a separate column, list the principles or activities that you value most in life. What matters the most?

- Out of the qualities you listed, circle those that are of greatest importance.

- Answer the following questions: How could you make your life better? How can you help your family? What could you do better at work? How can you improve your relationships? What could you do differently to nurture your friendships? What can you do to improve the environment?

- Why do you want to live more simply? Are you in debt? Are you stressed out? Is your home a mess? Do you spend enough time with your family? Do you hate your job?

- What is your ultimate goal? One way to nail down your goal is to envision your perfect day. What does it look like? How is it different from the way you spent today?

- Now that you have a handle on what you value and what your mission is, craft a concise minimalist statement that captures your intentions.

- Condense your minimalist statement into a couple of sentences. Use no more than 25 words.

- Revisit your mission statement every three months. Evaluate your progress and make adjustments that continue to mirror your minimalist mission.

Common Mistakes

1. Your minimalist statement is too lengthy. Mission statements are short and concise. One or two well-crafted sentences are all you need.

2. You are focusing on the small stuff when you need to see the big picture. You may want to spend less on coffee or declutter the living room. These are stepping stones on the path, but they aren't the destination. Why are you employing minimalist philosophies? What are you going to gain?

3. Your minimalist statement is too vague. Don't overgeneralize. Be specific. What do you want? Happiness is a great goal, but what does happiness look like from your perspective? What do you need to be happy?

4. It is full of fluff. Be straightforward and say what you mean. It doesn't have to flow perfectly or use big words; it just has to be authentic.

5. Your statement sounds good, but it isn't what you really want. Your minimalist statement should resonate with every particle of your being. If you cannot connect with your mission, then you need to return to the drawing board. What is it about minimalist that attracts your interest? What inspires you?

Allow yourself to aspire towards greatness. Your minimalist statement should inspire you to move forward, work hard, and create changes. It adds context to your journey and the choices you make. A clear vision of what you desire provides the motivation you need to go the distance. Take charge of your life right now. Connect to your purpose, and write a few words that convey your mission.

"Have nothing in your houses that you do not know to be useful, or believe to be beautiful." **-William Morris**

What Do You Really Need?

Owning less can bring far more joy than having to organize it all. In Buddhism, it is thought that material things hold us down and create unnecessary suffering. Nothing lasts forever, and yet we grow attached to objects that eventually fail, bringing frustration, anger, or sadness. Many would say that there is too much emotional attachment to things in general. It clouds your perception of what is truly important. If you do not need a house full of shiny objects, what do you really need? Minimalists focus on this question, holding on to no more than what is necessary to sustain a happy, healthy life.

If you are like most people in today's culture, you are buried in belongings. Each year you buy and accumulate more and more objects. How often do you let a few things go? Do you ever feel like you do not have enough space to put it all? You might think that the solution is to buy more and bigger containers to create some sense of organization. Next year there will be more birthdays, more holidays, more vacation souvenirs, new fashion trends, faster electronics, and more sales. You could just pile it on top of last year's heap. Organization is a temporary solution to a life-long problem. Year after year, you continue to pack these things away in the basement, attic, or garage. You move the stuff around, but it never really goes anywhere.

Accumulating clutter can negatively affect your mood. It can lead to panic, mood swings, depression, frustration and stress. When left to grow, these negative emotions begin to manifest physically as weight gain, relationship struggles, problems at work, or even physical disease. Clutter can lead to a chaotic and troublesome life. Fortunately, the opposite can be said of a clean, uncluttered space.

What purpose do these objects serve? Who is benefitting? If you have something in storage for over a year, then the truth is that you really don't need it. You can invest time and money in storage solutions all day long, but whose life is seeing improvement? It may be time to face a harsh and selfish reality. You have all these things packed away, meanwhile someone down the street may be in dire need of them.

Organization is not the solution, but there is another option. You can change your perspective. You can free yourself from the burden altogether. You can save time, spend less money, gain free time, and even work less simply by changing your definition of what you need. Minimalist living means you begin to value experiences and relationships over material wealth. You can find happiness without a teetering pile of possessions.

Re-evaluate your life. Instead of rearranging, really look at your material things. Think about your goals and your passions. Focus on your minimalist statement. Let go of anything that serves no purpose to you or your mission. Removing unnecessary objects lightens your load and allows you to move forward more quickly. It frees up time that can be spent on more pleasurable pursuits.

Selling items can fatten your bank account. You will gain physical space to move and grow. Having less to maintain will reduce stress. Donating to charity or gifting to a friend will make you feel good inside. Removing the cutter will allow you to focus more attention on more powerful rewards. By giving up the material objects you gain freedom, joy, and room for new opportunities. If you are ready to gain all of this and more, then begin by letting go of one object at a time.

Getting Started:

- Start with five large boxes or bags.

- Label one bag for trash; this is where you will put worn objects with no use left.

- The second should be for selling. These items should be in excellent shape and have plenty of use left.

- A third bag can hold treasures you think your friends or family members could put to good use.

- A fourth box or bag will hold the things that belong elsewhere in your home. Use this particular bin honestly.

- The last is for donations that can be brought to your local church, goodwill, or second-hand store. These items are new or gently used, but still have some life left.

- Make it fun by challenging yourself to make the biggest donation pile possible.

- Stay energized by opening a window to let in fresh air and playing your favorite music.

- Reduce your debt by selling items that are in like-new condition. Use the money to make a credit card payment or pay back a personal loan.

- Unused items still bearing a price tag can and should be returned to the store.

- Release anything that does not serve a purpose or add something vital to your life.

- Some items will have an emotional hold. Try to separate from these feelings from the item itself. Getting rid of something will not make the memories vanish.

- You do not have to let go of a lot all at once as long as you make the effort and see the value of making this change.

- Promise to stop and think before making a purchase. Is it something you really need? If not, leave it at the store.

One of the most important virtues of minimalist living is to consume and maintain less. Eliminating clutter is a huge step in the right direction. You will soon feel a huge weight begin to lift off of your shoulders. Once your space is cleansed, you can begin to reevaluate the choices you make and start to transform your life. The process can be emotional, therapeutic, enlightening, and empowering. You can try it right now. Pick a space in your home. Look at the items it holds. Evaluate each from your new perspective. What can you live without?

"You have succeeded in life when all you really want is only what you really need."

–Vernon Howard, 1918

Practical Decluttering Tips: Room-By-Room

You have already learned the merits of living with less. Now it is time to explore tips that will assist as you begin to declutter your kitchen, bedroom, bathroom, living room, and office. Maybe you are ready to get going, but you still aren't quite sure where to start. Each room provides its own opportunities and challenges.

As suggested in the previous chapter, start with four or five boxes assigned to donations, garbage, gifts, relocations, or storage. Begin with mini goals and keep pecking away until your entire house is clear of distracting objects. You likely won't be able to get through it all in a single day, or perhaps not even in a week. However, you can make a dent. There's no better time to start than the present, even if you only have five minutes. You can always do another five minutes tomorrow and the next day until it is done.

Each object you come across will require a firm decision. Some of these will be quick and simple while others may bring significant soul searching. If you get stumped, revert to how recently you have used the item. If it has been more than a month, and it isn't a seasonal object, then you can probably live without it. If it has been a year or more, then you definitely don't need it. Be sure to take care of trashed or donated items immediately to prevent second guessing.

As you continue your minimalist journey, revisit these tips to ensure your space stays clutter free. One of the easiest ways to do this is to take 10-15 minutes each week to revisit each room and either relocate or discard anything that is out of place.

Kitchen

The kitchen is one of the easiest places to start. Being a more function-focused room, you won't find many sentimental items here.

- Begin with clean counters and take care of any stray dishes. Fill the sink with soapy water so you can wash up dusty items quickly before placing them back on the shelf or into one of your sorting boxes.

- Start working on a single shelf inside a single cabinet. Stay focused.

- If you find an object that goes elsewhere, group those items in a box so you can put them away later.

- Expired food goes in the trash, no exceptions.

- Recycle any piles of plastic shopping bags you have sitting around.

- Inspect your spices, eliminate multiples. Consider buying a spice rack to keep you organized if you don't already have one.

- Don't forget the junk drawer.

- Designate one drawer or basket for mail.

Bathroom

Bathrooms tend to be fairly simple as well. If you have more than one, evaluate some of the contents together to prevent acquiring too many multiples of products.

- Limit each bathroom to two bottles of your favorite shampoo, body wash, lotion, etc. This should include one open bottle and one back up. If you feel the need to stockpile larger quantities, store them in a separate location so you can manage your inventory more easily.

- Store samples in a single basket and use them immediately. If they haven't been used within a month, it is time to donate them.

- Discard expired medications immediately.

- Round up all those half-bottles of product that have been sitting around for months, if not years. If you like it, make a point of using it up. If you don't, trash it and remind yourself not to buy more.

- Evaluate your towels. Discard or repurpose any worn out ones that you no longer use.

- As with products, limit yourself to two brushes, combs, nail clippers, curling irons, and so forth, if you actually use them. If you never use your hair dryer, for example, consider donating it.

Living Room

In addition to being relaxing and comfortable, you want your living room to be presentable. This is the most popular location for entertaining guests. As you declutter, consider both function and aesthetics. You might find you need an extra-large bin for stray items this time around.

  – Walk around your living room. Pick up everything and anything that is not in its designated spot. Set this bin aside for now.

- Begin further decluttering by evaluating one area of the room at a time. Determine what you do and don't need.

- Purchase small bins or baskets for groups of items that tend to be used in the living room, such as remotes, magazines, or your children's toys. Keep these items well-organized. Having designated spaces helps you recognize how much you already have and prevents you from buying more.

- Straighten the books on your bookcase. Gift or donate any you don't plan on reading again. Do the same with magazines.

- Keep throw blankets nicely folded and limit the room to just a couple. Extras can go in your linen closet or be given away.

- Your living room probably looks pretty nice now. Return to that large bin from the first step. Decide which items to return to their proper locations or discard into one of your four sorting bins.

Bedroom

Your bedroom should be your sanctuary. Anything that distracts from your ability to get a good night's sleep needs to leave.

One common mistake is keeping a TV in the bedroom. Yes, many people like to watch TV in bed, but research has shown that keeping your viewing out of the bedroom leads to a more restful and relaxed night's sleep. Try moving your television into another room.

- If your bedroom is small, place the sorting bins just outside your door.

- Empty your end tables and only return the essential items, such as a flashlight or the book you are currently reading.

- Nothing should be on your bed besides pillows and blankets.

- Make certain to remove anything work-related from your bedroom.

- Keep dirty clothes in the hamper. Store clean clothes in your closet or folded in a bureau. Be diligent about keeping these boundaries.

- Gift, sell, or donate any clothes that you have not worn in the last year.

- Store jewelry in your jewelry box and nowhere else.

- Maintaining a clean and tidy bedroom will save you time and money.

Office

You will be surprised how much more focused and motivated you will become when your home office is clean, organized, and free of clutter. Your boss will likely notice too.

- Schedule decluttering sessions to prevent excuses from interrupting your decluttering plans. Schedule fifteen minutes a day until the job is done. Then, maintain your space by doing a quick review, preferably at the end of each week.

- Another way to ensure your office stays clutter free is to hang a reminder in a visible location: "Keep it Simple".

- Keep two small bins on your desk. Assign each of your projects a single file folder inside your "to do" bin. The second bin is for things that need to be filed. Don't let this bin pile up.

- Group like things together. Place paper and notepads in one drawer. Keep all of your pens or paperclips in separate cups or drawers.

- Eliminate pens that don't write, pencils that lack erasers, or broken staplers.

- Shred paperwork that you no longer need.

- Keep the top of your desk neat and clean. If you don't use it every day, it doesn't need to be there.

- Minimalism doesn't have to being boring. Choose stylish organization bins. You will be more likely to use them.

Decluttering your entire home is a big job. Start out room-by-room and zone-by-zone. Over time you will notice a big difference. Once the bulk of the work is done, you can kick back and enjoy the rewards. Just a few minutes of maintenance at the end of each week will ensure you stick with your minimalist principles. Release some of the weight you have been carrying around by eliminating the physical stuff that holds you back. It's worth repeating. What can you live without?

Find More Time

Are you constantly rushing around? You might feel like all of your time is consumed by working, commuting, shopping, cleaning, or running errands. You are probably right. Wouldn't you rather spend your time relaxing, getting quality sleep, engaging in hobbies, or interacting with your family members? It sounds good, but where will you ever find the time? You may think that there just aren't enough hours in a day to get everything done. Adopting a minimalist mind-set can help you find those missing hours.

When you adopt a minimalist lifestyle, you will begin to value your time above everything else. By budgeting your time carefully, you will discover the time you need to build the life you desire. Your life should be focused on the important things, like pursuing goals and nurturing relationships. Start trading your time for happiness, not money.

Psychologist and happiness researcher Sonja Lyubomirsky explains that your perception of happiness is affected by several factors. Your genetic makeup represents about half of your happiness quotient. Meanwhile, your finances, looks, and health take up only 10% altogether. As much as you might love your job, it is probably not the real source of your happiness and neither is the money that it brings. Lyubomirsky contends that the remaining 40% is decided by you and how you manage your life.

When you carefully manage and prioritize your time, your stress levels begin to drop. Conversely, when you do not manage your time well, it gets consumed by mundane and unfulfilling activities. You begin to feel overwhelmed and undernourished. You might start to miss deadlines or skip sleep to get it all done. You are in a constant battle against the clock. Your personal relationships suffer because you are tired, stressed, and irritable.

In addition to being over-scheduled, you likely have a few time-wasting habits. These are activities that you use to unwind or distract yourself without any tangible rewards. You might have a habit of talking on the phone, playing video games, texting, watching television, window shopping, or browsing various webpages for hours at a time. While these can be enjoyable and relaxing, it is also common to devote more time on these activities than you intend. Before you know it, an hour or two have passed. This is fine if you have absolutely enjoyed those two hours. However, if you feel as though those two hours were lost or wasted, then it is time to set limits. Try limiting yourself to 15 or 30 minutes. Set a timer. Put the remaining time to good use.

You shouldn't waste your life doing things you don't enjoy. According to *Becoming Minimalist*, "Nobody really believes happiness is directly tied to the number of things we own. Yet almost all of us live like it. We work more hours than ever before, earn more income, but save less. Personal debt has increased dramatically over the precious three decades. And consumer spending has been exalted to a virtue." Through minimalism you can reduce your spending and eliminate debt.

You can reduce the amount of money you need to live and the number of hours you need to work. You can also use minimalist strategies at work to get more done in less time. Follow the steps below to achieve all of this and more. Soon you will find ample time for enjoyable activities that promise a true sense of personal fulfilment.

How to Find More Time

- Recognize that life is to be enjoyed.

- Before committing to any activity, consider its pros and cons. How will it benefit you? Will it bring you closer to your minimalist statement?

- Learn to be assertive. Say no. Do not commit yourself to unnecessary or unpleasant activities.

- Ask for help. You do not have to do everything yourself. Delegate to get the job done faster.

- Keep a meticulous and organized calendar. Listing everything you must do allows you to identify free time.

- List your tasks in order of priority so you know what to do first. You might even find low-priority tasks that can be eliminated completely.

- Take advantage of small chunks of free time. Listen to music, read, or go for a walk.

- Be efficient and remove distractions. Focus on getting the job done. Consolidate tasks and errands whenever possible.

- Cut unnecessary expenses so you can work fewer hours

- Don't procrastinate. Do your work now to avoid having to handle things twice.

- Beware of time wasters and set limits. Don't blow half your day checking your email or watching television.

If you are not happy doing things the way you are doing them, then stop. If you cannot stop entirely, at least become more efficient so you can spend less time doing them. Put yourself first. This is your life, you should enjoy it. Start simplifying your life so you can stop being so chained to the clock. Work and other commitments might be necessary, but they should not take precedence over your happiness or your family. Effective time management will allow you to slow down and live your life. Stop doing what you are supposed to do. Instead, start making time to do the things you want to do.

Just Say 'No'

The 'Just Say No" slogan doesn't only apply to drugs or teenage peer pressure. Saying "no" is an important life skill. To maintain your minimalist lifestyle, you will need to develop the ability to say no to certain invitations, gifts, or requests without feeling guilty. Make healthy choices by rejecting anything that interferes with your minimalist statement.

Has this ever happened to you? You've had a long, stressful day at work. You are ready to go home and kick your shoes off. Just as you are counting down that last ten minutes, your boss saunters over and pleads for you to stay to complete an extra project. He entices you by hinting that overtime hours come with extra pay. Even though you really don't want to stay, you might agree because you don't want to let your boss down. This is a decision that you immediately regret, but it's too late to reconsider now.

Maybe it isn't your boss that you have trouble saying no to. Perhaps it's a friend who is always asking for rides, a co-worker who invites you to grab lunch at an overpriced deli every day, or a family member who monopolizes your weekends. What all of these scenarios have in common is that they are making demands on your time. Minimalist statement aside, it is essential to your psychological health that you develop the strength to say no, taking control of your time and, ultimately, your life.

The Right Wording

Encouraging you to say no is all well and good. However, this discussion would be meaningless if it weren't accompanied with some guidance on how to say no tactfully. You want to reclaim your time and say no to clutter without alienating your friends or aggravating your boss. You can become so skilled at saying no that everyone feels as though they have benefited in some way.

Say 'No' To Your Boss

To illustrate this point, turn you attention back to the work example where your boss was requesting that you work extra hours. This is a common scenario, and often the worker feels pressure to relent. Respond to your boss' query by presenting a quantity versus quality assessment. Suggest that everyone would benefit if you continue to focus on your current project or assignment before accepting additional work. Taking on too much might hinder your ability to do well.

Examples:

- "You know I would like to accept, but at the moment all of my attention is focused on completing _____ to the best of my abilities. If I take on a new project, I won't be able to complete both in a satisfactory manner."

– "I would like to. However, I am currently really swamped. Let me know if you want me to adjust my priorities."

The second example empowers your boss by allowing them to choose which project receives your attention while also establishing that you are only able to complete one of the tasks.

Say 'No' To Friends or Family Members

You might find it more difficult to say no in your relationships with friends or family members. If you are too busy to go to dinner or visit the theatre, you will need to make your choice clear without offending them. You don't want them to feel as though you don't want to spend time with them. At the same time, you don't want to spend too much time or energy stressing over how to say no.

1. As a rule of thumb, you should always start by genuinely thanking them for the invitation.

2. Tell them you are unable to attend.

3. Offer an alternative at a later date. Ideally, this would be something that requires less of your time.

Examples:

- "I appreciate your invitation to Aunt Meg's birthday celebration. I am too busy on that date, but I will send a gift. I hope you have a wonderful time."

- "Thank you for offering. I can't make it to the charity lunch myself, but I've invited several people. You should have a great turn-out."

By phrasing your "no" this way, you make your rejection clear without offending anyone. Your friend or family member cannot be sore as you are clearly still contributing in your own way. Give it a shot next time you are invited to do something that you would rather not. *Offer thanks, say "no", and present an alternative.*

"There are two ways to be rich: One is by acquiring much, and the other is by desiring little."

–Jackie French Koller, 1948

Spend Less

Nothing complicates your life more than money. Pursuing money steals your time. However, having too little money steals your joy and creates stress. Marketing PhD Emily Garbinsky contends that "When it comes to managing finances, it's easy for people to feel overwhelmed and out of control." Minimalist living simplifies your finances. By spending less, you can feel more financially secure, pay off debt, and save for a better future. Garbinsky contends that the quickest way for consumers to get control of their money is to feel empowered in the decision-making process. So how can you become empowered?

First, you will need to change the role of money in your life. Somehow it has become more important than it should be. Money cannot buy happiness. You don't need to make a lot of money if you can spend less. Money is a means, but it is not the only way to find bliss. Value your time more than money or the things it can buy. Before you make a purchase, evaluate the price in terms of your time or freedom rather than dollars or cents. Do not spend money unless you are going to gain something valuable in return.

According to Gallup research, two out of every three Americans does not have a personal spending budget. It is not surprising then that debt is at an all-time high. Bankrate's Greg McBride contends that over 30% of Americans are on the brink of financial ruin, carrying more than $15,000 in credit card debt. It is easy to spend too much when you have no idea how much spendable income you actually have.

Two basic spending rules can eliminate your need for credit cards. The first rule is to only buy what you absolutely need. The second is to only spend money that you have. If you are currently carrying credit card debt, put these two rules into action. Free up more cash and pay off those cards as quickly as possible. Having a credit card payment is not an essential expense. By paying these down, you will find more money in your wallet at the end of the month. Focus your energy on breaking the debt cycle. You need to spend less than you make.

Financial advisor Laura Shin recommends a 50/20/30 approach to minimalist spending. In this approach, your essential expenses, such as rent, heat, electricity and food, should make up no more than 50% of your budget. If you are spending more than 50% of your monthly income on essentials, then it may be time to downsize. Reassess what you really need versus what you can do without. 20% of your budget should go towards financial obligations and investments. This is where you put the credit card payments, savings account deposits, and retirement investments. This is the part of your budget that will allow you to enjoy minimalist living indefinitely.

That should leave 30% of your monthly income for discretionary spending. These are things that are not essential, and will not aid your future, but make life more comfortable today. Cable, internet, cell phone bills, entertainment, gym memberships and impulse buys all fall into this category. If these items make up more than 30% of your budget, then you should sit down and decide which expenses add value to your life, and which waste your time and money. Be bold and cut as many expenses as possible.

Simply spending less money may seem like an oversimplification. In truth, the answer is easy but the action can prove quite challenging. Fortunately, the challenge will fade once scrutinizing purchases becomes a habit. You will need to take a close look at your income and assess how much you really have available to spend.

Some expenses are unavoidable. You have to pay your rent or mortgage if you want a place to live. Others have some flexibility. In truth, you could probably spend less on groceries, clothing, entertainment, or coffee. After you have taken care of the essentials, realize how much is left over for discretionary spending. Start creating new habits that allow you to spend as little as possible.

How to Spend Less

- Establish a budget, pay off debts, and cut unnecessary expenses.

- Opt out of consumerism. Stop viewing shopping as a form of entertainment. Embrace joy from other sources.

- Choose less expensive forms of entertainment. Visit the park instead of the mall. Invite friends over for coffee instead of meeting at the local café.

- Unless you need something, stay out of the stores. They are designed to encourage impulse buys. Find more fulfilling and budget friendly activities to fill your time.

- Use cash. Cards make it too easy to overspend.

- When your weekly cash allowance is gone, stop spending.

- Think before making a purchase. Ask yourself whether it is something you need or want. Be honest.

- Create a 30-day wait list. Write down any non-essential purchases. You will likely find that the urge to buy vanishes by the end of the 30 days.

- Look for freebies or try borrowing one from a friend before buying your own.

- Check second-hand listings before buying new furniture or appliances.

- Get creative. You might be able to make it yourself for a fraction of the price. Bonus: You'll get a boost of pride and confidence.

- Have fun. Don't focus on all the things you will go without. Make saving money your new source of entertainment.

Putting the brakes on spending can be a challenge, but it is one you can easily overcome. Take an honest look at your income and spending habits. Decide what you really need to live and thrive. Create a budget that allows you to flourish without being wasteful or accumulating debt. Your future self will thank you for the sacrifices you are willing to make today. Make smart choices. Before you make your next purchase, ask yourself whether that pair of shoes or upgraded phone is worth your freedom. By spending less, you will actually gain more time, pleasure, confidence, and security.

"Simplicity involves unburdening your life, and living more lightly with fewer distractions that interfere with a high quality life, as defined uniquely by each individual."

–Lina Breen Pierce, 1947

Downsize to Save More

According to Carmella Ferraro's "Small but Perfectly Formed" feature in *Financial Times*, the average home size in 1950 was 1,000 square feet or 92 square meters. In 1978, the average home was 1,700 square feet or 150 square meters. A strange thing has happened over the last few decades. Although the average family size has fallen, the size of homes has continues to rise to an all-time high of 2,000 square feet or 180 square meters. This wasteful trend is attributed to a rise of wealth and consumerism.

Minimalists looking to conserve money and natural resources while enjoying a freer, more authentic lifestyle are beginning to rebel against the status quo. The current movement towards smaller living is growing in popularity as the cost of living continues to soar. What began as fringe movement indulged only by eccentrics now represents 1% of new home purchases.

In the aftermath of Hurricane Katrina, architect Matianne Cosato began designing small shelters that could provide the same convenience but greater comfort than the miserable FEMA trailers. In 2006, her 300-square-foot cottages sparked the attention of both eco-conscious minimalists and thrifty resort owners.

The most dedicated minimalists release nearly all of their possessions to live in tiny homes, buses, or vans. While you don't have to live out of your car to adopt a minimalist lifestyle, their choices provide an interesting solution. Imagine if you could live better in less space. Imagine how much more you would enjoy life if you could support all of your needs on a mere $7,000 a year. The options for tiny living are many. You could test the waters by buying a smaller home or renting a smaller apartment.

While downsizing is both ecologically friendly and financially sound, it does come with its own set of challenges. Whatever new home you choose, you will be forced to eliminate a lot of material things that you plainly do not need. Your focus will turn to survival and creativity. You will find that, when forced to do with less, many of your belongings can fulfil a multitude of purposes. Successful downsizing requires careful planning and some serious thinking outside the box.

To avoid cabin fever, you will want to choose a location where the weather and neighborhood are favorable to getting outside and enjoying the fresh air. There are also storage issues, which will require you to eliminate cutter and hone your organization techniques. Zoning laws can also work against tiny homes that don't meet new construction minimums and are not always welcome at RV parks. Vouching for the movement's popularity, the American Tiny House Association was founded in 2015, ready to help eliminate red tape obstacles to minimalist living.

With zoning kinks resolved, you can focus on the benefits of extreme downsizing. Your bills will shrink. Your rent or mortgage will be smaller, as will all of your utilities. It costs far less to light and heat a smaller space. It will be easy to curb your shopping additions and spend less money because you know you do not have any place to put unnecessary items. You can work less and enjoy nature more, conserve resources, and revel in self-sufficiency. You can spend less time cleaning or maintaining and more time relaxing and enjoying life. Your family dynamics should improve too. In a smaller space you will find more opportunities to enjoy each other's company. If your new house is on wheels, you can relocate in a pinch and travel without ever leaving home.

Downsizing is emotionally freeing. Don't let the strain of a large, taxing home prevent you from living the kind of life you want. Your home should be your greatest asset, not your biggest source of stress. Start planning your transition to smaller, simpler living now.

- Evaluate your life and determine if downsizing is right for you.

- Explore all of your options. Be honest about what you can afford.

- Involve the whole family. Talk with your children about the possibly of sharing a room.

- Set a realistic timeline and make it happen.

- Make a list of the items you need to survive. Go over this list at least twice. Scratch off anything that you can live without. This is your packing list.

- Remember that you do not need doubles or backups. One is enough.

- Get creative to ensure a level of privacy.

- Eliminate unnecessary belongings. Sell them or give them away. Keep only the absolute essentials.

- Choose furnishings that multitask. A futon can act as a bed and a sofa. An ottoman can offer seating and extra storage. A small desk can be your workspace and your dining table.

- Organize the move. This should be easy since you are only moving the bare essentials.

Downsizing could be exactly what you need. It is okay if you still aren't sold on composting toilets or sleeping, eating, and working in the same space. You can still downsize without going to an extreme. Choosing a smaller home or apartment will shrink your bills, pay off debt, slim down your work load, and improve your relationship with your family members. Take the opportunity right now to decide if downsizing is right for you.

"Fear less, hope more; eat less, chew more; whine less, breathe more; talk less, say more; love more, and all good things will be yours."

-Swedish Proverb

Eat a Healthy Minimalist Diet

Good food is one of life's simple pleasures. Yet, all too often it is overcomplicated. You want to make nutritious, earth-friendly choices without spending too much money. Even after you decide what you want, you still have to go to the store, bring it home, cook it, eat it, and then tidy up your kitchen. The trick to simplifying meal time is to adopt a minimalist philosophy in regards to food. Opt for basic, clean, unprocessed foods, and buy only as much as you need.

The minimalist diet is not a food fad or weight loss plan. It is simply a way to approach food from a different mind-set. That said, you may find that you do look and feel better after adopting a minimalist diet. That is because the focus is on nutrient-dense, whole foods. Minimalists eat real food.

The minimalist diet has many of advantages. It is easy to prepare, inexpensive, and better for your health. It places less strain on the environment. Simple, whole foods don't require large, air-polluting factories to be run or maintained. They don't need extravagant packaging that ends up in landfills and pollutes our water. Fresh foods tend to be sourced closer to home, which means lower transportation costs, less wasted fuel, and fewer carbon dioxide emissions. While your personal choices may not save the planet alone, you can rest assured that your diet is not adding to the strains. Your minimalist diet will also allow you to spend less time cooking or planning meals. The minimalist diet is also very delicious.

Most minimalists cut out overly processed foods filled with dyes and unknown chemicals, and so should you. Processed foods are a bad investment. Most are a waste of your money as they devoid of the nutrients your body needs. They harm your health which can steal time and happiness. Research conducted by the Dana-Farber Cancer institute suggests a clear link between the consumption of processed foods and an increased cancer risk. Mayo Clinic contends that processed foods typically contain high levels of sugar and sodium which can cause diabetes, high blood pressure, and heart problems.

Simple food is not bland or boring. Natural foods are full of flavor that you might miss out on if you choose complicated preparations. Save time and energy by preparing your food as simply as possible. Fresh fruit can be eaten whole or sliced and drizzled with honey, or maybe grilled for a few minutes. Bright orange carrots make a nice crunchy snack. Wholesome vegetables can be steamed or roasted with a little olive oil, salt, and pepper. Greens can be tossed with chopped herbs and a spritz of vinegar. Proteins can be seared and presented with a simple sauce or some fluffy brown rice.

Preparing foods more simply creates a more enjoyable kitchen experience. You won't need to clutter your counter space with an array of appliances. A cutting board, a knife, and couple of pans should see you through. There is less to think about or juggle. You aren't running around trying to get everything together, instead you can revel in the beauty of an heirloom tomato and savor the scents wafting from the roasting pan.

It also discourages overeating. Minimalists conserve resources. Binge eating is wasteful and bad for your health. According to studies conducted by Brown University, binge eating can create weight gain, heart problems, high blood pressure, and a host of psychological challenges. Simple, minimalist food preparations will slow your mind, allowing you to savor every bite rather than shoveling it all down. When you plan to consume only as much as you need, you leave more room for pleasure.

One of the biggest ways to take the stress out of meal time is to plan ahead. Don't waste your time or gas money making several trips to the grocery store every week. Instead, plan out simple meals for the entire week. Making a careful list allows you to know what you need. Then, you won't buy extra produce that will be left to wilt in the bottom drawer. Don't buy it unless you are going to use it.

Following the steps below will assist you in spending less time and money at the grocery store. They will help you stress less, waste less food, and enjoy a healthy minimalist diet. The key is to become mindful of the food choices you make and the way they impact your life and the earth itself.

Getting Started

- Keep it simple. Look for quick and easy recipes with three ingredients or less. Choose basic ingredients that don't need a lot of partners.

- Make a plan before you head to the grocery store. Know what meals you are buying ingredients for and how long they need to last.

- Limit frozen foods and dining out. Paying someone else to make your food increases the costs and complicates the process.

- Avoid processed foods. Processed foods are bad for your health. Choose healthy, wholesome foods.

- Make substitutions. Don't cut out the junk without replacing it with healthy, less-wasteful alternatives. Grapes, apples, and carrot sticks are simple, convenient snacks.

- Make an effort to consume less. Eat enough to sustain a healthy body, but don't overindulge. Conserve resources as much as possible.

- Only buy as much as you need. Count your produce to prevent spoilage. Don't buy it if you aren't going to use it.

- Know that purchasing in bulk doesn't always save money. Factor in the monetary cost, shelf life, club fees, and the storage space needed.

- Avoid packaged foods as much as possible. Packaging is wasteful, adds unnecessary costs, and is bad for the environment.

- Don't buy bottled beverages. Drink water instead. It is healthier, requires no packaging, and saves you money.

- Limit alcohol consumption, or avoid it altogether.

A minimalist diet is an easy way to add more joy to your life. You eat three times a day. That is three opportunities every day to use less and enjoy more. Don't waste another chance to improve your life. Adopting a minimalist diet won't just boost your mood; it can also improve your health, fatten your pay check, and help save the environment. Start today by making your next meal simple, stress-free, and delicious.

"The simplest things are often the truest."

–Richard Bach, 1936

Save Water

Minimalist living is all about conserving resources. Water is one resource that is particularly essential to your life. According to Mayo Health, you need to drink 0.5 gallons, or 2.1 liters of water each day to support basic body functions. That is literally a drop in the bucket when it comes to daily water usage. The average home actually uses closer to 250 gallons every day, which amounts to nearly 100,000 each year. That is not counting the water used to grow food or manufacture the consumer goods we purchase.

When it comes to conserving resources, this is a huge problem. In fact, the United States Environmental Protection Agency has been warning of "water-stress" conditions since 1990. These conditions have continued to worsen over the past decades to the point that the warnings now include 45 of the 50 states. It is a problem that communities are seeing in nations throughout the developed world. Making an effort to conserve water in your home will save you money while helping to improve a global problem.

Research conducted by the National Academy of Science found that on average Americans use more water than the people in any other country. According to Indiana University's Assistant professor of the Department of Public and Environmental Affairs Shahzeen Attari, people tend to grossly underestimate their water usage. American's in particular underestimate their usage by 100%, which is to say that they use twice as much as they think they do. Attari warns that while you might assume that water is a bountiful and renewable resource, that isn't exactly the case. Studies show that the world's clean water resources are dwindling due to climate change, overpopulation, and poor management.

Fortunately, changing your water wasting habits can be just as easy as underestimating your usage. You need to become more aware of how much your home really uses. Find your latest water bill. Divide the total usage by the number of days it covers. The divide it again by the number of people in your household to estimate how much water each person is using.

Sadly, about half of the water you are billed for is flushed right down your toilet. A single flush uses between 5 and 7 gallons of water. Showers, washing machines, and landscaping also waste significant amounts.

Another big source of water waste is a meat-based diet. While not required, many minimalists adopt vegan or vegetarian diets. According to the Water Footprint Network, it takes more than 1,800 gallons of water to produce a single pound of beef. In contrast, producing a pound of tofu requires less than 300 gallons of water. Although water is still being used, the savings are certainly significant.

While installing more efficient fixtures and appliances can help, you really don't have to spend a lot of money in order to significantly reduce the amount of water you use. Small behavioral changes can really add up. In the water conservation battle, every little bit really does help. You can cut your consumption by more than 30% by enlisting the steps below.

- Check your pipes and faucets for leaks and have them fixed immediately. Even a small leak can waste upwards of 20 gallons in a day.

- Always turn off the tap while you are brushing your teeth, shaving, or scrubbing your hands.

- Take shorter showers.

- Replace your faucets and showerheads with low-flow versions. With an average cost of $30, your new fixtures can help you save upwards of 45 gallons of water every day.

- Consider installing a low-flow toilet to cut your water consumption in half.

- If you cannot replace your toilet, consider adopting this slogan from the 60's: "If it's yellow, let it mellow." Or, place a brick or tank bank in the back of your toilet.

- Don't use your dishwasher or clothing washing machine until you have a full load. One large load uses less water than multiple small loads.

- Don't bother pre-rinsing your dishes.

- Collect and use rainwater to water plants or wash your car.

- Start a compost bucket instead of using the garbage disposal.

- Research and install low-flow aerators. These can be purchased for just a few dollars and installed in seconds without any special tools.

- Choose drought-resistant landscaping plants.

- Keep a pitcher of water in your refrigerator for cold drinks instead of running the faucet until it is cooled.

- Consider adopting a vegan or vegetarian diet.

Conserving water is perhaps one of the easiest things you can do to reduce your carbon footprint. Get your entire family in on the act by educating them on the simple ways they can save gallons of water. You can reduce your bill, conserve resources, and even reduce pollution all by making a promise to become more mindful of your water usage. You can take the first step right now by maintaining awareness of the amount of water you use throughout the rest of the day. Let that awareness begin to change the way you look at water.

"You may have occasion to possess or use material things, but the secret of life lies in never missing them."

–Gandhi

Conserve Fuel

Perhaps the largest hurdle you will face in your quest for minimalist living will be to reconsider your mode of transportation. Owning and driving an automobile is ingrained in society. An abundance of advertising assures you that owning and driving a new vehicle is the fastest route to freedom. Sleek sports cars and aggressive pickups might be sexy, but they are also are expensive, often-dangerous machines that are ruining the earth. More importantly, they perpetuate your dependence on a dwindling resource.

The world you live is far more dependent on oil then most people care to acknowledge. You have to commute to work every day. Errands must be run. Goods must be transported to stores so that you can purchase them. Everything from food and clothing to toys, electronics, tools, and mail is shipped on trucks that require fuel. There are three main problems with this situation. It costs a lot of money, it damages the environment, and it places strain on a finite, non-renewable resource. It is a situation that cannot continue without dire consequences.

Despite an undeniable awareness of the problem, the world's consumption of oil continues on an upward trend. According to the United States Energy Information Agency, the United States alone uses more than 134 billion gallons of gasoline every year, breaking down to 368 million gallons every day. That is just one country. Collectively, the world uses 85 million barrels of oil every day. That is nearly 3 billion gallons every single day. All of that oil has to come from somewhere and that source is being depleted faster than it can ever be replenished. If you own and drive a traditional vehicle, then you likely consume between 600 and 1000 gallons of fuel every year.

You have probably heard crude oil referred to as a fossil fuel. That is because crude oil is formed from the decomposition of dead organisms deep beneath the bedrock where it encounters both heat and pressure. It is a natural process that takes hundreds of millions of years to occur. Needless to say that once we run out it will be gone for good. Estimates by leading experts indicate that there is only enough fossil fuel to last a single human lifetime at the current rate of consumption.

Not only is the current dependence on oil and gasoline not sustainable, but it is also wreaking havoc on the environment. Both traditional gasoline and diesel release pollutants including carbon dioxide into the air, which many scientists agree contributes to climate change. You have likely seen coverage of the large-scale, wildlife-killing, water-polluting oil spills that are becoming more and more frequent—not to mention that the processes used to harvest and refine crude oil are harmful as well.

Are you ready to get serious about your fuel consumption? You may not be able to give up your car entirely, or buy a new electric model, but there are many steps you can take to save gas. Most of these tips will also save you time and money. To get started you will have to become more mindful of your oil consumption. Stop taking gasoline for granted. Limit your usage as much as possible. Changing your mindset can be a struggle, but putting your new commitment into action couldn't be easier.

- Drive less often. Skip nonessential trips, combine errands, and make a real effort to schedule appoints more efficiently.

- Consider taking public transportation. Do some research; you might be surprised by the abundance of choices in your area and the amount of money you could save.

- Carpool with a neighbor. The Natural Resources Defense Council estimates that gas usage could decrease by more than 30 million gallons if each commuter vehicle carried just one more person.

- Riding a bike is more fun than sitting in a car. It is also cheaper and better for the environment. If you don't own a bike, do some research, your community might have a bike coop.

- Choose walking over riding for short trips. It is good for your physical and mental health.

- Get a more efficient vehicle. When you are ready to purchase a new car, opt for an electric hybrid. At the very least, choose the most fuel-efficient vehicle you can afford.

- Use smart driving techniques. Don't speed, tailgate, or leave your vehicle idling. Avoid stop and go traffic. Engage cruise control on the highway.

- Stay on top of care maintenance. Properly inflated tires and a finely tuned engine will improve gas mileage by a combined 8%.

- Don't waste time or fuel circling the parking lot.

- Reduce evaporation by tightening the gas cap and parking in the shade on hot days.

Minimalist living relies on certain values like consuming less, being self-sufficient, saving money, making earth-friendly choices, and conserving resources. Nothing about oil dependency is minimalistic. Imagine what your city would look like without so many vehicles on the road. Consider how not having a vehicle would affect your life. What changes would you have to make? Would you find the swap personally rewarding? Driving less would also mean spending less money, perhaps working a few less hours, and breathing cleaner air.

Take action right now by vowing to reduce your oil dependency. The first step you choose could be as easy as picking one day a week to forgo driving anywhere. Continue looking for simple ways to reduce your fuel usage during the other six days.

"Here is your country. Cherish these natural wonders, cherish the natural resources, cherish the history and romance as a sacred heritage, for your children and your children's children. Do not let selfish men or greedy interests skin your country of its beauty, its riches or its romance."

–Theodore Roosevelt

Be Energy Conscious

A recent study from the Energy Information Administration shows that energy use is continuing to increase. The report goes on to explain that this is happening despite a rise in the cost of electricity and rising affordability of energy efficient products. If you are like the average consumer, then your household likely uses more than 900 kilowatt hours of electricity every month. The electricity delivered to your home is made using fossil fuels, coal, wood, or natural gas. If you hope to conserve resources and reduce your electricity bill, you will have to do more than choose an energy efficient television.

The failure to reduce energy use despite significant measures can be attributed to two problems. First, while new homes are more energy efficient, they are also being built, on average, 30% larger than older homes. Secondly, according to the Washington post, people are consuming more and larger electronics which, while energy efficient, all rely on electricity resulting in greater electric consumption overall. Stay conscious of the amount of time you spend plugged in. In addition to wasting energy, iPads, televisions, cell phones, and computers clutter your life and remove you from your environment.

The solutions seem simple enough. You could choose the smallest home or apartment possible, resist buying all the latest tech gadgets, get a smaller television, and limit screen time. These are all good steps, but is it enough? Minimalist living strives to reduce your consumption to the bare essentials. These steps are a good start, but there still more that can be done.

Become more conscious of the amount of every your home uses. Familiarize yourself with your electric meter and regularly study your electric bill. If you want to significantly reduce your consumption without sacrificing modern conveniences, then it is time to consider alternative energy sources. Green energy is more sustainable, cheaper, and better for the environment.

If you are able to make an upfront investment, consider creating your own energy. Installing a few solar panels or a wind generator will allow you to make your own clean energy. Living off the grid is an attractive notion to most minimalists. You will be more self-sufficient and less vulnerable to outages when the grid goes down. You can still maintain an electric backup in case something goes wrong. However, as long as your system is functioning you can kiss your electric bill goodbye.

You might not be ready for wind or solar, but you can still make small changes that will go a long way towards making your home more energy efficient. First you will need to look at the structure of your home itself, the bare bones. Inspect your windows, roof, and the inside of your walls. Most homes can benefit from new energy efficient windows, a little foam insulation, or a new roof. These things can go a long way in conserving heat and therefore reducing the amount of electricity used through an oil furnace, electric heater, or air conditioner.

While you are at it look, at your lighting options, electronics and large appliances. First, evaluate which ones you could live without all together. For the minimalist, less is always more. If you cannot live without, see if you can afford to swap them out for more efficient models. Consider using a gas-powered stove. Electric ovens are huge electricity hogs. Once your home is made more efficient, it will be time to reduce your personal energy usage. Below is a list of ways to cut your energy use.

- Stop wasting electricity. Avoid redundant lighting and flip the switch when you leave the room.

- Sell or donate electronics and appliances that you don't really need.

- Go a step further by unplugging electronics when you leave.

- Make unplugging electronics easier and faster by installing strip cords.

- Swap incandescent bulbs for compact fluorescent or LED Bulbs, which last longer and use less electricity.

- Opt for wind, solar, geothermal or natural gas over electric energy.

- Air dry your laundry on a clothesline whenever weather is agreeable.

- Put on a sweater instead of turning up the heat.

- Open your curtains to let in natural sunlight instead of turning on a light.

- Before turning on the air conditioner, try sipping a cold beverage or opening a window to let in a breeze. If you must use it, be conservative with the temperature setting.

- Make your home more efficient by addressing air leaks.

- Clean the coils on your refrigerator twice a year to make sure it is running efficiently.

- Consider applying solar landscaping.

- Limit screen time as much as possible.

- Adjust your thermostat before leaving home.

Reducing your energy use will lower you bills, conserve resources, and preserve the environment. While some of the steps to becoming more energy conscious can be rather costly, changing a habit is free and produces immediate results. The best thing you can do for the environment is to remain conscious of the amount of energy you use and make a genuine effort to use less. Begin by making a list of the things you can do to make your own home more energy efficient.

"But I deal with this by meditating and by understanding I've been put on the planet to serve humanity. I have to remind myself to live simply and not overindulge, which is a constant battle in a material world."

-Sandra Cisneros, 1954

Reduce, Reuse and Recycle

Adopting the three R's is essential to minimalist living. In order to be a minimalist, you must reduce your consumption, utilize what you have to the fullest, and discard what's left in such a way that it can find new purpose. Nothing should be wasted. This cycle is good for your bank account, the planet, and your community. While you are probably already familiar with the three R's, it is time to start taking them seriously. Have you ever stopped to think about where your garbage goes after it leaves your bin?

As consumerism has risen, so has the amount of waste created. In the 1960's, the average person produced just under three pounds of waste in a day. Despite the advent of recycling and the 1970s environmental movement, this figure has continued to grow. According to Duke University's Center for Sustainability and commerce, the average person now generates more than four pounds of waste every day. That adds up to nearly 90,000 pounds being created by you in your lifetime. As a global community, a recent report by the World Bank shows that our planet's population produces an estimated 2.6 trillion pounds of garbage every year. All of that garbage has to go somewhere.

To take a closer look, the United States alone collects over 220 million tons of waste every year. Despite the now prevalent presence of recycling centers, the Environmental Protection Agency confirms that more than half of that waste is still being buried in landfills. Collectively, those landfills account for more than 20% of the country's methane gas emissions. Resources are being wasted, and the planet is being destroyed.

Getting a handle on your consumerism can help. Minimalist living is living with less. When you buy less and use less, you will also waste less—thereby reducing the amount of garbage your household generates. Get a handle on your waste by being more conscious of what you buy. Think twice before putting anything in the waste bin. With a little creativity, you might find that most things have another purpose. When all else fails, make sure you discard unusable waste in a responsible manner.

Recycling solves many problems at once. In addition to safeguarding the environment, eliminating landfills, and repurposing waste, recycling stimulates the economy. Studies by the United States National Resource Defense Council determined that recycling a ton of waste creates twice as many jobs as burying a ton of waste in a landfill. The same ton delivers nearly $300 worth of goods and services, $100 in salaries, and $140 in sales to the economy. It also saves energy. For example, recycling one ton of plastic nearly 6,000 kilowatt hours of energy and 700 gallons of oil. Recycling one ton of paper saves 4,000 kilowatt hours of energy, almost 400 gallons of oil, and at least 17 trees.

The three R's really can make a difference. However, in order to make the process work, you have to complete the cycle. Buying less is great. Reusing items is awesome. Recycling is vital. However, there is a fourth step that is often overlooked. In order for recycling to be an effective solution, you have to choose recycled products when you make a purchase. Not doing so breaks the cycle and continues to waste resources.

If you look, you will find and abundance of products made from recycled materials. When you must make a purchase, seek these out. According to statistics from the Environmental Protection Agency, if every American family chose one roll of recycled paper towels over one conventional roll, then the net result would be the preservation of more than 500,000 trees. Imagine how many trees could be saved if only 100% recycled paper towels were available, or if you stopped using paper towels altogether.

Get motivated to reduce your waste by keeping track of the amount you generate in a week. Accept responsibility for your role in the mounting trash problem and take action. Respect the earth by respecting its resources and using them wisely. Use the easy steps below to reduce the amount of strain you place on the planet.

- Don't buy it unless you really need it.

- Before you make a purchase, consider the waste that will be generated. Opt for less packaging whenever possible.

- Choose recycled, earth-friendly products.

- Opt for reusable containers over plastic bags or wrappings.

- Instead of purchasing disposable water bottles, purchase a reusable bottle and fill it yourself.

- Before putting anything in the recycling or waste bin, ask yourself whether it can be used for another purpose.

- Use glass jars to store dry goods or organize craft supplies.

- Fix broken items instead of discarding them. If you don't have the time or ambition to fix them, gift them to someone who does.

- Donate cardboard boxes and tubes to local schools for craft projects.

- Start a compost to make use of organic materials and create nutrient dense soil for your garden

- Know what your local center recycles. Don't send anything that isn't accepted, it will end up as waste.

By reducing, reusing, and recycling you can conserve resources, stimulate the economy, protect the planet, and better your community. Challenge yourself to significantly reduce your landfill contributions. Stop buying what you do not need. Stop wasting resources. Minimalist living is about enjoying what you already have. Try to complete the rest of your day without creating any waste. It might take some serious thought, but you can do it.

"Be content with what you have; rejoice in the way things are. When you realize there is nothing lacking, the whole world belongs to you."

–Lao Tzu, 500 BCE

Enjoy New Forms of Entertainment

Minimalist living is all about simplifying your life so you have more time. Now you just have to figure out what you will do with all of that free time. You may find it difficult to fit your favorite pastimes into a minimalist mindset. Hobbies can be expensive, messy, time-consuming, and even chaotic. A recent article in the Journal of Psychosomatic Medicine suggests that hobbies can also be great for relieving stress, preventing work burnout, and staving off depression.

Minimalism shouldn't be seen as a restriction. You do not have to stop doing everything you love because it doesn't fit into your new minimalist lifestyle. Instead, consider this as an opportunity to expand your horizons. Look for ways to make old hobbies more sustainable, and add new ones that you can enjoy and feel good about.

Playing electric guitar may not be essential but if it is something you truly enjoy, then you should continue. Just stay mindful of the amount of money you are spending and the amount of electricity being used. On the other hand, if you have a large collection of yarn that you haven't touched in years, then you should honestly consider whether knitting is really right for you. It might be better to find someone who will put those boxes of yarn to better use. This will free up space to adopt a hobby that better suits you.

Fortunately, there are loads of activities to choose from. Minimalist forms of entertainment are great for everyone. They do not take up a lot of time or money. They require little to no travel, so you won't waste fuel or pollute the environment. There are social events for extroverts, solitaire hobbies for introverts, and a wide range in between. A study conducted by the National Cancer Institute shows that enjoying a leisure activity can add up to five extra years to your life. Explore the tips below to find a minimalist activity that is right for you.

- Check your local paper or bulletin board to scope out free local events. Small concerts, farmers markets, and trade shows are especially popular during the summer months.

- Use the internet to find deals on hobby supplies or activities before paying full price.

- Remind yourself that having a hobby is not a license to hoard. Limit your supplies to a certain area, say one shelf or one box. Stop buying when it exceeds that boundary.

- Invite a group of friends over for a weekly potluck or game night.

- Choose a local park or hiking trail and pack a picnic lunch.

- Take up gardening. It is a pleasant activity that will add to your minimalist diet and reduce trips to the grocery store.

- Rent or download a movie instead of traveling to the theatre. It is cheaper and better for the environment.

- Choose a crafting hobby that uses sustainable materials, such as basket weaving or wreath making.

- Instead of buying more books, visit the local library.

- Learn how to play an instrument that doesn't require electricity. Example: acoustic guitar, drums, fiddle, violin, xylophone, or trumpet. Buy used if possible.

- Take up a physical activity. Running, walking, yoga, and biking are cheap, fun, eco-friendly, and good for your health. Try new routes or postures to keep it interesting.

- Head to the nearest beach. Most public beaches are free to visit.

- Watch the sun rise or set with a loved one.

Don't waste your entire life watching television or buying more stuff. While those things can be enjoyed in moderation, overdoing it distracts from your purpose. Remember your minimalist statement? Instead, get out in nature and enjoy the world that you are working so hard to preserve. Or invest your time in something you value, like quality family time, friendship, art, literature, or music. Devote yourself to activities that bring you bliss. It doesn't really matter what you do as long as it adds pleasure to your life. Start taking full advantage of your free time.

"The consumption society has made us feel that happiness lies in having things, and has failed to teach us the happiness of not having things."

–Elise Bouling

Redefine Happiness

After you strip all of the excess from your life, you will begin to experience a new kind of happiness. It happens without financial or material wealth. All that extra stuff is not what adds value to life. When it is gone you will start to notice and appreciate the simple things again. In the end happiness is about gratitude, not greed. Minimalist living means having and spending less, but the net gain is actually an ability to do and experience more. A study performed by Van Boven and Gilovich showed that consumers gain more happiness when they buy experiences than when they purchase material things.

This is not a new concept, and yet so many people fail to make use of this knowledge. Money and things don't make you happy. Research has verified this fact over and over. One of the first studies on the topic was conducted in the 1970's by P. Brickman. In that trial, lottery winners were compared with a control group made up of people whose salaries were just barely enough to cover their basic expenses. Brickman found that the millionaires weren't any happier than the members of the control group.

More recent research conducted by Dunn et al sought to explain this observation. They discovered that happiness is affected by how you spend your money more than it is affected by how much money you actually have. In particular, the study found that people felt happier after purchasing a gift than they felt after purchasing something nice for themselves.

Happiness is strongly tied to the relationships in your life. From an evolutionary perspective, people need to work together and form a mutual understanding in order to survive as a species. Love brings more happiness than a bigger TV or a faster car. It makes sense then that experiences bring more joy than possessions. Experiences are often shared with others, either physically or through storytelling.

Neurologically speaking, adopting a simpler lifestyle can create happiness. When you experience something new, you begin to feel excited. As you start to adopt a minimalist lifestyle, and change various aspects of your life, your brain responds to this excitement by releasing feel-good chemicals called endorphins. As you continue making changes that allow you to work less and play more, those endorphins will continue to flow. Minimalism is a great mode for establishing a more authentic sense of happiness because it creates more opportunities to have exciting experiences.

In essence, there are two kinds of happiness. There is a superficial and temporary form of happiness that comes with owning a large house, making lots of money, wearing fancy clothes, buying a nice car, or having hundreds of television channels to choose from. All of these things come with strings and obligations that can make life stressful, challenging, and cumbersome.

The second type of happiness is more genuine, lasting, and profound. It comes from loving relationships, fulfilling careers, and enjoyable leisure activities. This kind of happiness permeates your life when your basic needs are met. When you experience real happiness, you will no longer need the mountain of material things that previously distracted you from your unfulfilled life.

If you are unhappy and you feel as though you have already tried everything to change your situation, then you are left with only one option. You must change your expectations. Minimalism helps you do that by removing all of the clutter that you expected to make you happy. Instead, you are forced to confront life with just the essentials, which means that you become responsible for your own happiness. Happiness is an internal emotion that only you can control. In order to discover the happiness you deserve, you need to create the change you wish to see.

– Establish healthier habits that nurture the truest, barest sense of yourself.

– Accept yourself despite your personal limitations.

– Don't expect happiness to come from material gains.

– Look at your life and the things that you own. Discard the bad. Own and appreciate the good.

– Think about the way you spend a typical day. Does it make you happy? If not, start putting minimalism into action so you can spend more time doing the things you love.

- Think about your relationships. Let yourself appreciate the good they add to your life.

- Make a conscious effort to spend more time helping others.

- Spend your money on experiences, not material things.

- Accept that, while your life may not be perfect today, you are indeed moving in the right direction.

- Practice gratitude.

When you decide to be happier with less, you free yourself from the chains of consumerism and open your life to a whole new level of happiness. When you welcome gratitude into your life, you will begin to discard any jealousies or insecurities that may have clouded your emotions in the past. Accept yourself and your station in life. When you can accept a life with less, you make space for more fulfilling experiences. There is more joy to be found in living life, than can ever be bought inside a shopping mall. Stop chasing happiness with money. All you really need is a new perspective.

Less Stuff Means More Freedom!

Material wealth prevents you from being free. Constantly working to buy and maintain distracts from what truly matters. Owning more things can make you feel good initially, but it will also bring stress and anxiety. There is the stress of working to pay off debts. There is anxiety that you will miss a payment, or that a fire, flood, or burglary will take away your prized possession. There is the time you have to take from more enjoyable activities to clean, declutter, fix, organize, and store. It all has a way of dampening your mind, body, and soul.

When you break free of your possessions, you make room for happiness and joy. You can find the freedom of choosing how to spend your time and energy. Don't just declutter your home. Declutter your life. Free yourself from the strain of want. Stop feeling like you are lacking something and start embracing the simple side of life. Don't think of having less as a negative thing. Minimalism isn't about deprivation. Less truly is more.

– When you have less things to maintain, you can focus your attention on fun activities with people you love.

– When you have fewer things in your home, it will feel roomier and more comfortable.

– When you spend less money on unessential things, you can save more. This establishes greater security.

– When you have more money and fewer expenses, you will stress less.

– When you stop equating happiness to physical objects, you will begin to embrace the things that matter more, such as love, friendship, and experiences.

- When you stop wanting more things, you will experience greater freedom because you will not have to work as hard or as long to sustain your needs.

- When you stop overconsuming, you will relieve some of the strain on the environment.

- When you aren't held in place by a big house, overwhelming debt, or a mountain of stuff, you become free to travel the world.

The material things you have been conditioned to desire rarely add value to your life. More often they add additional complications. Where will you store them? How will you fix them when they break? In what ways are the latest gadgets and fashions distracting you from reality? Don't fear the discovery of empty space or time that appears when you eliminate material distractions. That emptiness is space for boundless opportunities.

For once in your life, you will be able to spend time with your family, travel, and pursue your hobbies. Fill your life with living, not more meaningless possessions. Be who you are, not what you have. It is an empowering experience. Question what truly matters in your life. What can you do without?

Getting rid of the clutter is liberating. Challenge yourself to give up something you think you need. Give away your favorite shirt, donate your favorite book, or give up your newest iPhone. See that you can continue to breathe and revel in the natural world. Happiness has nothing to do with the things you possess. When you have less, there is simply less to worry about. That is true freedom.

Enjoyed this Book? You Can Make a Big Difference...

Thanks for reading. I work hard to create useful and easy-to-follow guides for health and well-being, home and lifestyle improvements

If you found this guide helpful please leave a review. Positive comments make a world of difference to authors and other readers alike.

Thanks again.

J.N. LEE

Ready for More?

Discover how easy and practical Feng Shui can change your home today!

Feng Shui Fresh!

The easy new approach to make your home or office look and FEEL great!

The No.1 Feng Shui Download!

http://bit.ly/1UQQlFJ

FENG
SHUI
Fresh!

The easy new approach to make your
home or office look and FEEL great!

J.N. Lee

Copyright

Made in the USA
San Bernardino, CA
07 August 2016